U.S. ARMED FORCES

U.S. NAVY

by Allan Morey

pogo

Ideas for Parents and Teachers

Pogo Books let children practice reading informational text while introducing them to nonfiction features such as headings, labels, sidebars, maps, and diagrams, as well as a table of contents, glossary, and index.

Carefully leveled text with a strong photo match offers early fluent readers the support they need to succeed.

Before Reading

- “Walk” through the book and point out the various nonfiction features. Ask the student what purpose each feature serves.
- Look at the glossary together. Read and discuss the words.

Read the Book

- Have the child read the book independently.
- Invite him or her to list questions that arise from reading.

After Reading

- Discuss the child’s questions. Talk about how he or she might find answers to those questions.
- Prompt the child to think more. Ask: What did you know about jobs in the U.S. Navy before reading this book? What more do you want to know after reading?

Pogo Books are published by Jump!
5357 Penn Avenue South
Minneapolis, MN 55419
www.jumplibrary.com

Library of Congress Cataloging-in-Publication Data

Names: Morey, Allan, author.
Title: U.S. Navy / by Allan Morey.
Description: Minneapolis, MN: Jump!, Inc., [2021]
Series: U.S. Armed Forces | Includes index.
Audience: Ages 7-10 | Audience: Grades 2-3
Identifiers: LCCN 2019045470 (print)
LCCN 2019045471 (ebook)
ISBN 9781645274292 (hardcover)
ISBN 9781645274308 (ebook)
Subjects: LCSH: United States. Navy—Juvenile literature
Classification: LCC VA58.4 .M67 2021 (print)
LCC VA58.4 (ebook) | DDC 359.00973–dc23
LC record available at https://lccn.loc.gov/2019045470
LC ebook record available at https://lccn.loc.gov/2019045471

Editor: Susanne Bushman
Designer: Molly Ballanger

Content Consultant: Lieutenant Junior Grade Katherine Lindman, U.S. Navy

Photo Credits: U.S. Navy, cover, 3, 4, 5, 6-7, 8, 9, 10-11, 12-13, 14-15, 16, 17, 18-19, 20-21; DanielBendjy/iStock, 1 (foreground); turtix/Shutterstock, 1 (background); ART Collection/Alamy, 23.

Printed in the United States of America at Corporate Graphics in North Mankato, Minnesota.

TABLE OF CONTENTS

CHAPTER 1

SERVING AT SEA

A U.S. Navy warship speeds through the sea. It has large weapons. It is on **patrol**.

Navy Sailors make up the ship's **crew**. They keep the oceans safe. Sailors are at sea for months at a time. Everything they need is on the ship. There are barber shops, gyms, and stores!

fleet
cruiser
oiler
aircraft carrier

Navy ships often sail together in **fleets**. Destroyers and cruisers are small, fast warships. They protect other ships.

The largest ships are **aircraft carriers**. They are like floating airports! Fighter jets take off and land from their **decks**. Why? They can't fly across the ocean and back.

DID YOU KNOW?

Oilers bring supplies to Navy ships. Like what? They bring fuel to keep the ships running. They bring food, too! This happens about once a week.

CHAPTER 2

NAVY JOBS

New Navy members are called **recruits**. First, they go to boot camp. They must pass physical tests. These include swimming tests.

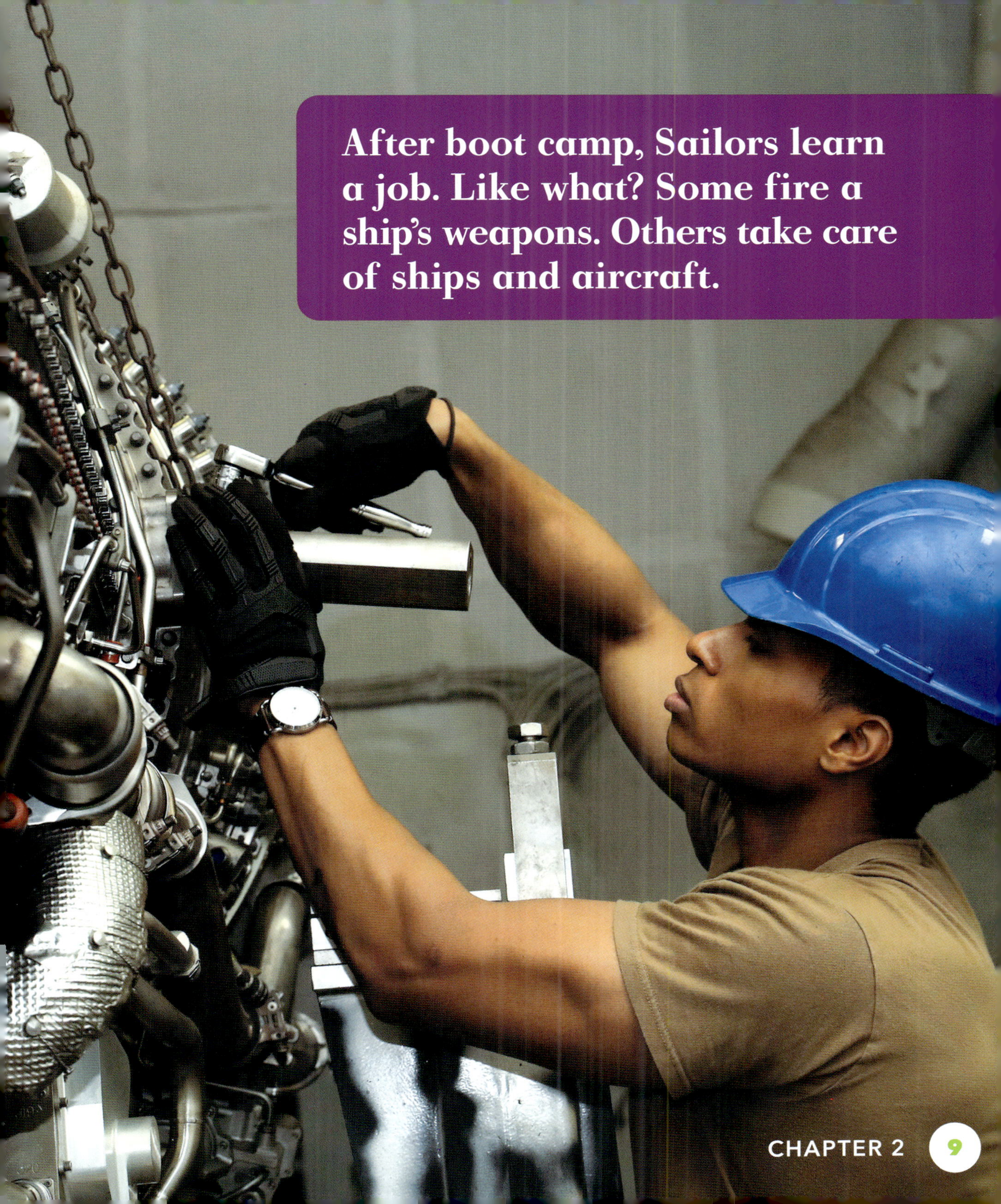

After boot camp, Sailors learn a job. Like what? Some fire a ship's weapons. Others take care of ships and aircraft.

Some Sailors train to be officers. An officer might command one ship or an entire fleet. Others become pilots. They fly fighter jets and helicopters.

TAKE A LOOK!

Naval officers wear **insignia** to show their **ranks**. On formal uniforms, it goes on their shoulders. Take a look!

Admiral
This officer is in charge of a fleet.

Captain
This officer might be in charge of a ship or naval base or command warfare.

Commander
This officer could be second in command of a ship.

Lieutenant
This officer leads a group of Sailors.

Ensign
This officer just graduated from an officer program.

Some Sailors work in **submarines**. These boats can stay underwater for up to 90 days! Many are small. Sailors sometimes have to share a bed. They sleep at different times! They call this hot racking.

WHAT DO YOU THINK?

Sailors might be at sea for many months. How do you think this would feel?

submarine

Navy SEALs

Sailors can train to become Navy SEALs. SEAL stands for sea, air, and land. SEALs train to go anywhere on **missions**. They are highly skilled. They scuba dive underwater. They parachute from airplanes.

DID YOU KNOW?

In 2009, pirates took control of a U.S. ship in the Indian Ocean. Navy SEALs rescued the ship's crew!

CHAPTER 3

NAVY MISSIONS

The U.S. Navy works hard to keep the United States safe. It helps other U.S. military **branches**, too. During **conflicts**, Navy ships might carry Marines to shore. They use boats with air cushions. They are very fast!

Sailors bring supplies to **troops** on land. Navy helicopters carry hurt Army Soldiers to safety.

cargo ship

The Navy also works during times of peace. It patrols the oceans. It protects the United States from attacks by sea.

Navy ships keep **cargo** ships safe from attack, too. They travel with them across the ocean. They help keep the seas safe for all.

The Navy also helps during **natural disasters**. In 2010, an earthquake hit Haiti. The Navy sent hospital ships. Sailors on them helped hurt people.

Sailors help people around the world. Would you like to serve in the U.S. Navy?

WHAT DO YOU THINK?

The U.S. president is in charge of military forces. He or she is called the Commander in Chief. Would you like this job? Why or why not?

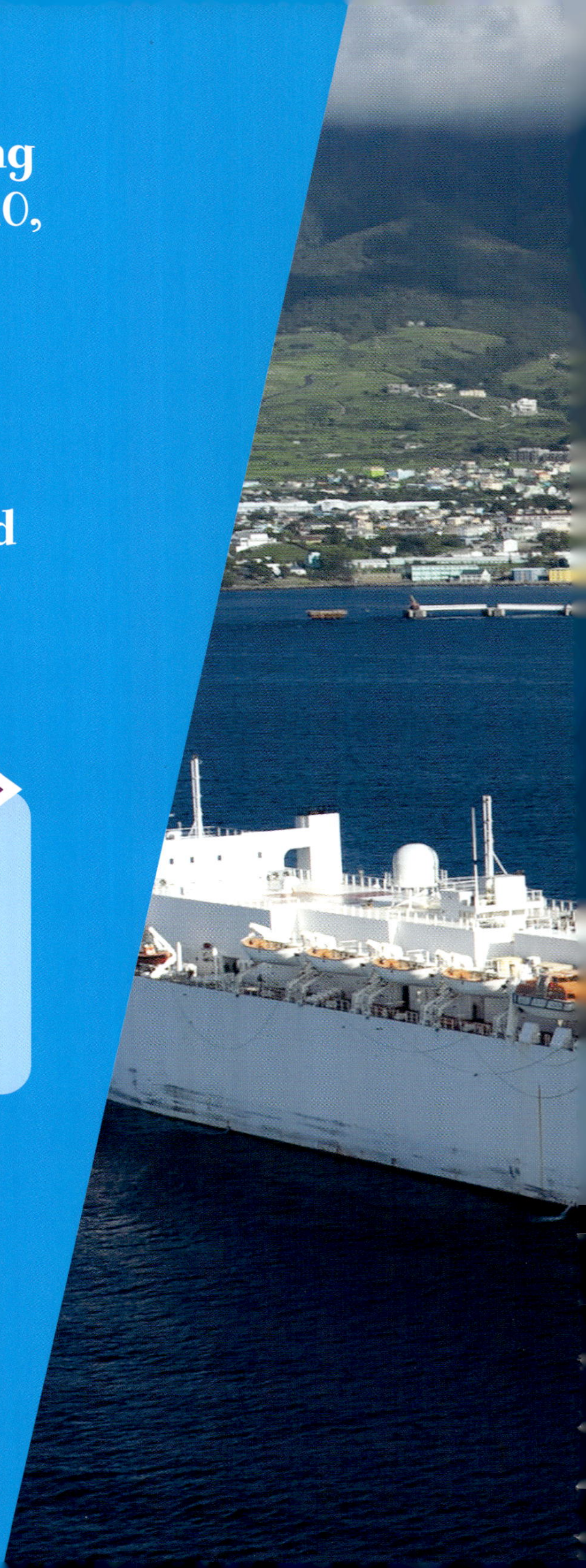

hospital ship

QUICK FACTS & TOOLS

TIMELINE

1775
The Continental Navy is formed during the Revolutionary War (1775–1783).

1776
The *Turtle* is the first U.S. submarine used in combat.

1920
The USS *Langley* is the first U.S. Navy aircraft carrier.

1962
The first SEAL teams are established.

1994
Women are deployed to combat ships for the first time.

U.S. NAVY MISSION
The mission of the U.S. Navy is to recruit, train, equip, and organize to deliver combat-ready naval forces to win conflicts and wars while maintaining security and deterrence through sustained forward presence.

U.S. NAVY ACTIVE DUTY MEMBERS:
around 332,000 (as of 2019)
Active duty members serve full-time.

U.S. NAVY RESERVE MEMBERS:
around 60,000 (as of 2019)
Reserve members train and serve part-time.

DEPLOYABLE SHIPS:
around 292 (as of 2019)

GLOSSARY

aircraft: Vehicles that can fly.

branches: The groups of the U.S. military, including the U.S. Air Force, U.S. Army, U.S. Coast Guard, U.S. Marine Corps, and U.S. Navy.

cargo: Goods and supplies carried on a ship.

conflicts: Wars or other fights.

crew: All Navy members working on a ship.

decks: The flat upper levels of ships.

fleets: Groups of ships.

insignia: Symbols that show the ranks of people in the military.

missions: Tasks or jobs.

natural disasters: Events in nature, such as hurricanes, earthquakes, and floods, that cause a lot of damage.

patrol: To keep watch over an area.

ranks: Positions in the military.

recruits: New members of a military force.

submarines: Underwater boats.

troops: Members of the armed forces.

INDEX

TO LEARN MORE

Finding more information is as easy as 1, 2, 3.

1. Go to www.factsurfer.com
2. Enter "U.S.Navy" into the search box.
3. Click the "Surf" button to see a list of websites.

FACT SURFER